lpeckskampeyahoo. com

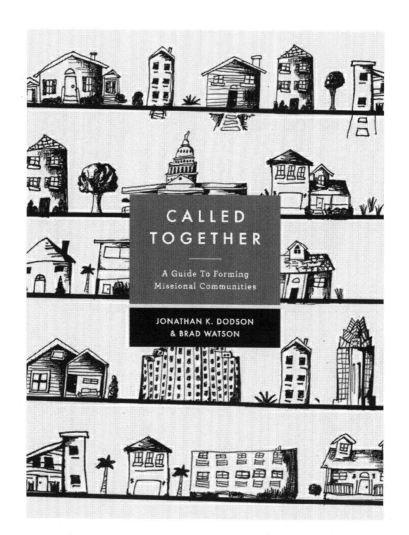

CALLED
TOGETHER

A Guide To Forming
Missional Communities

JONATHAN K. DODSON
& BRAD WATSON

CALLED TOGETHER

A Guide to Forming Missional Communities

JONATHAN K. DODSON
& BRAD WATSON

To City Life Church and Bread & Wine Communities

GCD Books is the publishing arm of Gospel-Centered Discipleship. GCD exists to publish resources that help make, mature, and multiply disciples of Jesus.

ISBN-13: 978-0692281734
ISBN-10: 0692281738

Cover design by Gretchen Jones Watson
Interior design by Mathew B. Sims

TABLE OF CONTENTS

INTRODUCTION   8
USING THIS GUIDE   11

    Week 0: **Starting a Missional Community**   14

PART 1: GOSPEL   20
    Week 1: **What is the Gospel?**   21
    Week 2: **The Gospel is Personal**   25
    Week 3: **The Gospel is Missional**   29
    Week 4: **Living the Gospel**   33

PART 2: Community   37
    Week 5: **What is Community?**   38
    Week 6: **The Defeaters of Community**   43

PART 3: Mission   47
    Week 7: **The Missional of a "Missional Community"**   48
    Week 8: **Being on Mission Together**   52

    Moving Forward: **Missional Commitments**   56

APPENDIX I: WEEKLY HANDOUTS   63
APPENDIX II: LEADERSHIP ROLE DESCRIPTION   74
APPENDIX III: LEADERSHIP DEVELOPMENT PLAN   76

ABOUT THE AUTHORS   80
OTHER GCD RESOURCES   81

INTRODUCTION

Everyone has a calling.

Many people spend years, even decades, trying to discover their calling. We try different jobs, experiment with hobbies, and volunteer for causes, all in pursuit of a call. Christians, however, know their calling the day they are born. We are conceived in the church and called to live *together*. While our secondary callings of vocation, family, and hobbies may vacillate, our primarily calling remains the same. Our roles as mothers and fathers, employers and employees, husbands and wives may change, but our calling as "saints together" remains the same (1 Corinthians 1:2).

Called Together

Describing the Church's calling, Paul writes, "God is faithful, by whom you were called into the fellowship of his Son, Jesus Christ our Lord" (1 Corinthians 1:9). We are called together in the fellowship of Christ. Christ is what we share together. This means the stickiness of our calling doesn't depend upon our proficiency but his glory and grace. Christ is what holds us together, through thick and thin. We live together because we are conceived together, in Christ. As a result, every Christian upon conversion is called into God's community. There are no exceptions. No one is left out. Everyone has a place in the people of God.

This calling of "life together" doesn't sit in the clouds. It is earthier. *How* we live together is of upmost importance. We are called to bear one another's burdens, be kind and tender-hearted, forgive one another, encourage one another daily, correct one another, counsel one another, comfort one another, teach one another, and serve one another *as saints together.*

Our collective holiness is a witness to our Holy God. How we live, then, not only expresses our calling but also narrates a story to the world. It tells others something about who Jesus is and what he is doing in the world. If our life together is focused on fulfillment from "one another," we will quickly devolve into a dysfunctional community marked by disillusionment, silent record-keeping, or unrealistic demands. We are called *into* community but not *for* community. We exist for Christ and in Christ. He is our all in all. If this is true, we will live together in a gracious, forbearing, truthful way. This way of living is a counter-cultural witness of Christ to the world. Our community becomes *part* of God's greater mission for us.

We are not only conceived in the church, but also called into God's mission—to redeem social ill, make good culture, and share a whole gospel. We are *sent together*, called to carry the good news to people and into cultures. You might recognize that our calling "together" is part of our collective mission. We are called and sent as saints together. As you'll see, there is an inherent tension in this calling. Sometimes Christ calls us into an experience of rich community that makes mission a byproduct. At other times, our pursuit of his mission creates richer community as a byproduct. Either way, mission and community overlap when Christ is the center. But when mission and community devolve into things we manage, they replace Christ as the center of our calling.

In an individualistic age of consumer church, our calling is often fumbled, confused, or even lost. How can we recover our calling to community and into mission? We believe missional community is a great way to live out our calling as *saints who are sent together.*

Missional Community

A missional community is a way to organize the church to gather and send groups of people on a common mission, (i.e. to engage artists in the city, renew your neighborhood, or help the homeless downtown). Simply put, missional communities are a group of people who are learning to follow Jesus together in a way that renews their city, town, village, hamlet, or other space. They aren't fancy. In fact, they can be a messy community of everyday citizens who are devoted to Jesus, to one another, to their neighbors and their city.

But what does this really look like? How should faith affect everyday life? How does church figure into our response to poverty and other social justice issues? What does evangelism and discipleship look like? Although buzzwords like "missional community" can be helpful or fun to talk about, many Christians simply don't know where to begin. We want to help you make it a believable reality.

Called Together is an eight week guide to help you learn together what it could look like to be a community of people who are devoted to God's mission. What would it look like if you took seriously your calling into Jesus, to one another, and to your neighbors and city? This guide will help you imagine and form a missional community that is true to your calling.

Our hope is that this discussion, mixed with application, will help you move from theory to practice, from good intentions to gospel action, from talking about "missional community" to becoming a "missional community." May the Spirit of God work out your calling by fashioning you into saints sent together, in Christ and for the world.

USING THIS GUIDE:
What to Expect

A *guide* is an informed book of elementary principles, an introduction to foundational concepts in a given subject. This is not the last word or an exhaustive explanation of missional community. Rather, it is intended to introduce and form missional community. We will cover the three foundational principles of missional community (Gospel, Community, and Mission), foster reflection on them through discussion questions, and guide you into making an informed missional commitment.

Preparation is Important!

Too often, we use curriculum like a microwave. Set the timer, push the button, and "bing" your community is ready. We hate to disappoint up front, but this guide can't produce instant missional community. You will need to prepare for this crucial and foundation laying season for your missional community. (Most worthwhile things in life require an investment.)

First, you will want to read through the entire primer before you start walking through it with a group of people. The order, discussions, and next steps are intentional and sequential. Be sure to follow along, and do the required work, so you aren't caught off guard, and so you can contribute to the growth of your community. Consider setting aside a regular time in your schedule to do this. You might do it with a friend, spouse, or your family.

Second, consider taking notes, jotting down good questions to ask, and be prepared to read sections aloud. Study the key passages of scripture, meditate on them, submit yourself to its authority. Spend time praying for the people in your community and the Spirit to open their hearts and minds.

Third, you may want to consider reading some supplementary resources to help you reflect more deeply on some of the concepts we introduce. While not an exhaustive list, we believe these will enrich your life, and help you live a more vibrant life *called together*:

- Ray Ortlund's *The Gospel*,
- Jonathan Dodson's *Gospel Centered Discipleship*
- Joseph Hellerman's *When Church Was a Family*
- Steve Timmis & Tim Chester's *Total Church*
- Brad Watson's *Missional Community Leader Guide*
- Jeremy Writebol's *everPresent Gospel*

How Each Week Works:

Here's what you can expect each week:

- **Big Picture:** This section provides three to four bullet points about the main ideas and purpose of each week.
- **Preparing to Lead:** This section will have some helpful tools and tips for leading each particular week.
- **Before the Discussion:** Your community is more than a discussion time. In addition to the discussion, this section will provide insight on how to creatively cultivate community each week. This will include vision casting, sharing stories, planning, and prayer.
- **The Discussion:** This is the heart of the guide. The discussion section has key passages, discussion questions, quotes, and important content *that should either be read aloud or closely paraphrased in your own words*. As you prepare each week, highlight questions you know will work well, and if necessary re-word questions to make them fit you.

    Perhaps the most important aspect of these discussions is the Bible. The Scriptures carry divine authority, and this guide is based on the truths of Scripture. Unlike anything that can be said or spoken, the Bible carries weight. The Spirit works through Scripture like lighten-

ing through steel to electrify our faith. It is fundamental
to forging conviction about missional community. Without it, we reduce church to best practices.

- **Later This Week:** From the very beginning, you will
face temptations to reduce missional community to a
meeting or a time-slot in the week. This section will provide next steps for your community to engage in being
called together, helping them take simple steps to apply
what they learn in your weekly discussions and times
together. Don't overlook this section! Read ahead and
plan so you can give people more than a few days notice
that you will be having a party, serving together, etc.
- **Handouts:** In Appendix I, you will find handouts you
can print for everyone in your community to take notes
on and follow along during the discussions. This can be
a helpful tool for groups or people who learn better this
way. The handouts also provide further study for each
individual to engage the content on their own, with
their spouse, or discipleship group.

WEEK 0:
Starting a Missional Community

Every missional community has three natural ingredients: qualified and called leaders, committed participants, and a shared mission in its city. "Week 0" is about prayerfully gathering leadership and committed partners who will journey with you as you become a missional community. This is a time of preparation and the best way to prepare is understand who the leaders are, and what they will be responsible for. This is also the time to invite others to commit to the journey of becoming a missional community.

As your community walks through this guide you will be lead to discussions about shared mission and committing together to demonstrate and proclaim the gospel on that mission.

Leading a Missional Community

As you begin dreaming about starting a community there are important questions to ask and prayerfully consider about leadership:

- Am I qualified and called to lead a missional community? Do I have capacity to be a leader? (See Appendix II for a leaders' role description)
- How do I need to grow as a follower of Jesus? (See Appendix III for a template and example of a leadership development plan)
- Who will lead alongside you? How will you invite them into leadership? How do they compliment your gifts?

Sharing Leadership

You cannot lead a missional community on your own. It takes, at minimum, five people to co-lead a community: a prayer leader, a meal coordinator, a host, a discussion leader, and a missional leader. A co-leader is someone who takes initiative for the discipleship of others. All the co-leaders are concerned and focused on creating an environment where people grow in the gospel and make disciples. Regardless of their specific role or gifts, leaders are thinking through how the community is going, they are taking initiative, and they are examples of the faith and repentance in the gospel.

You may be thinking: "Wow, five leaders? I only have seven people committed to this thing." Exactly. Missional communities require a team effort. Typically we view the leaders of our community group as the ones who serve, host, lead discussions, and create the environment for *us* to grow. However, any sustainable community that is on mission and sharing life will require a team of leaders. It will require people to operate in their gifts to serve and create an environment of gospel growth. This results in *everyone* in the community having a crucial part to play and submitting to one another in each role. Frequently missional community meals will look more like a leadership team meeting than topdown teaching.

There are many gifts. Co-leaders of a missional community will get together about once a month to check-in, pray, and work together on where the community needs to go next. During the first eight weeks, the co-leaders will guide discussions and help lay the foundation of this new community. Some leadership teams will put the responsibility of guiding the discussions on one leader who is gifted in teaching; however, all the leaders will want to work through this guide.

Leadership Roles in a Missional Community

Healthy communities share the load of being a community. Here are six important servant-leadership roles that ought to be filled by *different* people. There are many others, but these are the important ones to get started. Missional communities do not have "senior pastors," they have leadership teams.

- **Meal Coordinator**. You will want to delegate someone who likes to communicate clearly what the plan is for the upcoming week with the food and any other things coming up. Have this person communicate in whatever way is best for everyone (text, email, Facebook), about what to bring for the next meal, parties, service opportunities, etc. This leader needs to enjoy communicating in a friendly way, organizing, and delegating.

- **Prayer Leader.** This leader is responsible for calling the community to prayer, they lead prayer times, and are the spokespeople for turning the missional communities attention to asking God and listening to God. This person will organize and facilitate times of prayer. They will also share prayer requests. They are the leaders who are intentionally thinking through prayer in the life of the community.

- **Host**. Who can host the weekly meals? Who is blessed by having people in their homes and will think through creating a space that is conducive to sharing an intentional meal and discussion each week? The host ought to be a welcoming person who views their home as an outpost of the kingdom and space to share in gospel conversation.

  Being the host doesn't mean they clean up by themselves. From the very first meeting, invite everyone to pitch in with cleaning up after the kids, washing dishes, taking out the trash, and putting the home back the way it was when everyone arrived. Everyone participates in family chores! If your community treats the host family like a restaurant or catering service, you aren't cultivating community.

- **Discussion Leader/Facilitator.** Not all the leaders have to be skilled teachers or counselors. However, for the group to explore faith and obedience together, you will need a leader who can guide and lead discussions around the gospel, community, and mission. This guide will help the discussion leader the most. This leader enjoys teaching and explaining new truths as much as helping others engage those truths. They will be good teachers and good listeners, too. Their job isn't to preach, but to help others grow in their understanding of the gospel.

- **Missional Leader.** This guide builds towards the creation of a missional commitment with a shared mission. The shared mission of your missional community will be specific, relational, and regular. Meaning you will know who the people are, you will be able to get to know them, and you will serve and be around them often. The missional leader is the champion for the mission. This person is regularly reminding the group about the mission and why the group shares the mission. This leader's role is connecting the group to the mission and letting people know the next steps and opportunities.
- **Children's Coordinator.** If your missional community has young kids, you will want to have this leadership role. Who can organize the group to care for kiddos during the weekly discussions? This is usually as simple as someone making a calendar and having everyone sign-up. One simple method for structuring the kid's time is to have the adult leaders:
  - ✦ Teach the kids how to do something the leader is really good at (like play music, soccer, paint, cook, jump rope, etc.). It could be anything.
  - ✦ Share with the kids an important part of their story in learning who Jesus is and what he has done for them.
  - ✦ Share their favorite Bible verse and explain what it means and how it has affected their lives.

Inviting People into Missional Community

Before you start making phone calls and sending out invitations to start a missional community, take some time to think about *why missional community*. Why do you want to start one? Be honest with yourself. How would you describe a missional community in your own words? It's important that you describe it well as you invite people to participate. Your definition of a missional community should include: shared life, the gospel, care for the city and neighbors, and making disciples.

Think through what you are passionate about and who you are passionate about. Is it a neighborhood, a group of people, or specific names and faces you interact with everyday? What would a community that proclaims and promotes the gospel to them look like? What would it look like to welcome your neighbors into that kind of community?

Begin to pray for the people God will bring into that community. Pray for people to come alongside you and help. Pray for co-leaders and for God to connect you with others who have a similar passion. Pray for God to bring names to mind. Think through the specific people in your life you want to join your new missional community. They'll need to live fairly close to you since its hard to commute to community. You aren't looking for all-stars or elite Christians—they don't exist. Instead, you are praying about people who will commit to the process of becoming a community. Who will be teachable, humble, and honest in faith and repentance?

As you invite people, give them a picture of gospel-shaped community alive in God's mission. As you describe what you are prayerfully starting, avoid making your invitation tailor-made to each person, where you sacrifice your convictions. For example, you really want your friends who are struggling in marriage to join, so you tell them it will be a group that fixes marriages. Invite people into a community that isn't centered on their needs, hobbies, or passions but the gospel of Jesus and his mission.

Give Your Missional Community a Name

It doesn't have to be creative like a garage band, or spiritual, or from the Bible. However, your missional community needs a name or the default will be "Your Leader's Name Missional

Community." This unfortunately reinforces the idea that the community belongs to the leader, that it's their thing, and not our priority. Instead, set the tone from the very beginning by naming community together so it's everyone's community. To be sure, leadership is important and requires an increased level of responsibility, planning, and vision, but healthy communities are ones that get described as "our missional community." Some easy options are naming it after the neighborhood, sub-division, or even the street that will be the focal point for your missional community.

Set a Date and Get Started

You have a vision, a name, a team, and the logistics are working out. Now it's time to set a date for your gatherings and get started. Oddly, this can be one of the more challenging steps in the process. Eventually, you have to overcome the inertia of fear, anxiety, and spiritual warfare, and set a day to begin.

What Does a Weekly Gathering Look Like?

Generally, a weekly gathering begins with a shared meal for 30-45 minutes before transitioning into discussion, prayer, sharing stories, and so on. The sharing of the meal is an intentional time for people to connect and enjoy food together.

Even if people are still eating, it's okay to shift to a unified and intentional discussion. Plan to spend about an hour plus discussing scripture, praying, sharing stories and needs, or planning. The facilitator of these times carries the responsibility of moving things along.

Lastly, after you end your discussion and prayer, people will spend time cleaning up the house, washing dishes, and sometimes linger in conversation. Some of the best ministry can happen during this time!

GOSPEL

WEEK 1:
What is the Gospel?

Big Picture:
- Celebrate the beginning of something new and cast vision for the next eight weeks.
- Define the gospel *and* the three aspects of the gospel.
- Discuss how the gospel is doctrinal: changes what we believe.

Preparing to Lead:
The first four weeks are designed to get the leader and community on the same page, so they are foundational to everything else. As you can see in the table of contents, your community will spend four weeks on the gospel while only two on community and two on mission. This is because the gospel is critical to creating conviction, clarity, and common motivation in forming and sending communities on mission. It's easy for community, mission, or individual liberties to drift to the center of a community. These will derail the community and often lead to a false or shallow picture of the gospel.

Unfortunately, the gospel seems basic and elementary to most Christians. You will have to fight against this by really pressing people in the discussion times. As people share what they think are "obvious" answers, ask them probing questions like: What does it mean to believe? What is so evil? What is so wrong with us? What's so wrong with sin? Get past pat answers.

Before the Discussion:

You will also notice that the discussion content is shorter these first four weeks. This is intentionally designed to give your community time to *become a community*.

Before this week's discussion, share why you want to start a missional community. How did your journey lead you to this point? What were some key turning points? What do you hope to see happen? Why did you call this particular group together?

Invite everyone else to introduce themselves and share why they are wanting or thinking about being part of this specific missional community.

Following all of this, spend time in prayer for what is to come as you grow together. Pray like Paul in Ephesians 3:14-21.

Optional things to mark this beginning:

- Have a toast to this new beginning
- Have a "birthday cake."
- Take a group photo to commemorate the moment

The Discussion

Discussion Question: *What comes to mind when you hear the word "gospel"?*

The gospel is the good news that Jesus has defeated sin, death, and evil through his own death and resurrection and is making all things new, even us.

This definition of the gospel can be broken down into three aspects:

1. The gospel is *doctrinal*: it changes what we believe.
2. The gospel is *personal*: it changes who we are.
3. The gospel is *missional*: it changes where and how we live.

The Gospel is Doctrinal

Key Text: *"Now I would remind you, brothers, of the gospel I preached to you, which you received, in which you stand, and by which you are being saved, if you hold fast to the word I preached to you—unless you believed in vain. For I delivered* *to you as of first importance what I also received: that Christ died for our sins in accordance with the Scriptures, that he was buried, that he was raised on the third day in accordance with the Scriptures, and that he appeared to Cephas, then to the twelve." —1 Corinthians 15:1-5*

History-Making News

The gospel of "first importance" is the historic claim that Jesus Christ lived, died, was buried, and rose from the dead for our sins in the first century A.D. These events were anticipated in the Old Testament, witnessed in the first century, recorded in the New Testament, and attested by contemporary historians. In short, it is history-making news!

Discussion Questions:

1. *What does the gospel ask us to believe or receive?*
2. *Why is the gospel of first importance?*
3. *What are some other major history changing events, how do they compare to the gospel?*
4. *How does the gospel differ from the dominant beliefs of your city and culture?*

Christ-Centered News

Key Text: *Jesus says, "I am the resurrection and the life. Whoever believes in me, though he die, yet shall he live, and everyone who lives and believes in me shall never die." —John 11:25-26*

The gospel asks us to believe that Jesus died our deserved death (for our sins) and that he rose from the dead to give us his undeserved life (for our salvation). Notice that the "belief" required is not in an idea but in a person: "whoever believes in me." Jesus isn't asking us to merely agree with a doctrine, but to trust him for undeserved forgiveness and life. The gospel is Christ-centered.

In summary, the gospel is history-making, Christ-centered news that is so significant it bears believing and announcing. The doctrinal aspect of the gospel makes specific claims, grounded in historical events, which must be believed to know

Christ and receive his saving forgiveness. The gospel is not one spiritual idea among many. It is exclusive and unique in its claims because Jesus has uniquely done what none else can do (Acts 4:12; 1 Timothy 2:5-9)! *The doctrinal gospel changes what we believe.*

Discussion Questions:
1. *Do you believe the gospel? What is hard to believe about the gospel?*
2. *What do you find compelling or difficult about it?*
3. *What would the gospel be like without Christ at the center? Is that worth believing?*
4. *How do we, or our religious backgrounds, make the gospel about something besides Christ?*

Later This Week:
Split the group into two's or four's and assign each the job of meeting up later in the week to swap stories and get to know each other.

WEEK 2:
The Gospel is Personal

Big Picture:
- Sharing stories.
- Identity: the gospel changes who we are.
- Sanctification: how people change.

Preparing to Lead:

Again, you will be walking through material that some consider elementary. Probe the group with questions and be patient, allow silence, as people reflect on what it means to be truly changed?

The opening set of questions brings people into the tension of self-improvement or changing apart from the gospel. This week exposes your community to the idea that the gospel is not only a way into heaven, but a way forward into transformation.

Before the Discussion:

Have one of the leaders share their story. Have him share the defining highs and lows, the stars and scars. He doesn't have to go into the gory details of abuse or sin, but ought to be authentic instead of sliding the ugly parts under the rug. This first sharing of story is crucial because people will be watching and hearing for how honest this community will be. We tend to wrap up our personal stories with a nice bow. Instead, end with the present hopes and struggles to believe, trust, and walk with Jesus. This will also set-up the discussion well.

When the story is complete, open it up for a few questions and blessings. Then invite people to pray in response to what God has done in one person's life! Their story should be 15 minutes max, with 10 minutes to respond.

The Discussion:

Remember: The gospel is the good news that Jesus has defeated sin, death, and evil through his own death and resurrection and is making all things new, even us.

If we focus on just the doctrinal aspect of the gospel, we will neglect its other aspects. The gospel changes not only what we believe but also who we are. It is doctrinal and personal. It makes all things new, even us!

Discussion Questions:

- *Do you want to change? Why?*
- *What causes people to change?*

Key Text: *"And we all, with unveiled face, beholding the glory of the Lord, are being transformed into the same image from one degree of glory to another. For this comes from the Lord who is the Spirit." —2 Corinthians 3:18*

Beholding Jesus

The gospel changes us into the image and likeness of Jesus. Paul tells us that this gospel change happens by keeping our eyes on Jesus. It does not happen by keeping our eyes on our failure. The gospel frees us to admit our failures, because our worth doesn't hang on our success. Rather, our worth hangs on Jesus' success, his life over death. We can confess our sins without fear of judgment because Jesus has borne our judgment for us. As a result, for every look at sin we should look ten times at Christ, where we are reminded that Jesus is our forgiveness and acceptance before the Father. This kind of Jesus is worth beholding.

Discussion Questions:

1. Where do you look for approval? How do you hide your failures?
2. *Do you tend to look more at your failures or successes? Why?*
3. *How does the gospel adjust your perspective?*
4. *How does the Bible tell us people change?*

Becoming Like Jesus

The gospel offers hope because it gives us the eyes to behold Jesus as well as the power to become like him. The power for gospel change is the person of the Holy Spirit. The Spirit turns our eyes away from sin and toward our Savior. Because of the Spirit, we are transformed into the image of Jesus' glory:

> *". . . beholding the glory of the Lord, are being transformed into the same image from one degree of glory to another. For this comes from the Lord who is the Spirit"* —2 Corinthians 3:17-18

To be sure, becoming like Jesus is a life-long endeavor. This is why Paul mentions that we are changed "from one degree of glory to another." Our change is incremental and progressive. If we continue to look to Jesus, we will inevitably become like him.

The gospel changes who we are by changing what we look at. We become like Jesus because we behold Jesus. In summary, imperfect disciples cling to a perfect Christ while being perfected by the Spirit. Gospel change isn't perfection overnight but perseverance over a lifetime.

Discussion Questions:

- *How have you recently experienced gospel change?*
- *What does it look like to cling to Jesus Christ and be perfected by the Spirit?*
- *Who or what do you cling to when you sin?*

Later This Week:

Divide the group into completely different groups of 2-4 people and assign them the job of meeting up later in the week to swap stories and get to know each other. Challenge them to be open and authentic with their past, beliefs, and doubts.

WEEK 3:
The Gospel is Missional

Big Picture:
- Sharing stories again.
- Missional gospel: the gospel changes where live and what we say.
- Opening our eyes to see the transformation God is doing in the world.

Preparing to Lead:

This aspect of the gospel might seem the most foreign for your group. Isn't the gospel different from the mission? How does the gospel change the way we view the world? Doesn't it just change where I go when I die or how I view myself?

The straightforward answer is "No." The gospel doesn't just change your eternal destiny. It changes everything.

Before the Discussion:
Have another leader share their story. Again, pray in response.

The Discussion:

Remember: *the gospel is the good news that Jesus has defeated sin, death, and evil through his own death and resurrection and is making all things new, even us.*

If we just focus on the doctrinal and personal aspect of the gospel, we will neglect its missional aspect. If the doctrinal gospel changes what we believe, and the personal gospel changes who we are, then the missional gospel changes where we live and what we say. It is the hopeful announcement that God is making all things new in Christ Jesus! The gospel ushers us into a new kingdom and new world.

Key Text: *"The Spirit of the Lord is upon me, because he has anointed me to proclaim good news to the poor. He has sent me to proclaim liberty to the captives and recovering of sight to the blind, to set at liberty those who are oppressed, to proclaim the year of the Lord's favor." —Luke 4:18-19, Isaiah 61*

The Gospel Changes Everything

The gospel changes everything. It is not only good news for us, but also for our neighbors, the poor, our city, and the world. It affects the social, cultural, and physical fabric of the universe. In Luke 4, Jesus preached the gospel to the poor, marginalized, and oppressed. It is good news for them because through his death and resurrection he has defeated sin, death, and evil (1 John 2:13; 3:8). The gospel announces the in-breaking reign of Jesus, which is in the process of reversing the order of things. The poor become rich, the captives are freed, and the old become new.

Discussion Questions:

- *How does this aspect of the gospel make you feel? What does it sound like to you? How difficult is it to believe in a world like this?*
- *What are the visible signs of sin, death, and evil in our city?*
- *What would our city look like if Jesus reigned in our city?*

The Church Joins the Mission

Those who follow Jesus join his mission by making disciples of all ethnic groups and going, teaching, and baptizing (Matthew 28:18-20). We are sent to teach, speak, counsel, discuss, and proclaim the gospel to others so that they might be baptized into God's new creation and join his mission of making all things new. We are called "ambassadors of reconciliation" and given the privilege of sharing in Jesus' ministry of reconciling the world to himself (2 Corinthians 5:17-20). Those who have been changed by the gospel share its life-changing power with others. We should announce *and* embody the good news by caring for the poor and rebuilding cities (Isaiah 61:4). In fact, the future for the people of God is an entirely new city in a new creation (Revelation 21). The church should be a movie trailer of this grand, coming attraction, when all things will be made new!

Because the gospel changes what we believe and who we are, it should change where we live. We should make great culture, redeem social ill, and share a whole gospel. Christians should be among the most creative, neighborly, compassionate people in the city. If the gospel truly affects everything, then it should affect everything in our lives. It should change where we live. We will discuss this more in the mission section.

The gospel is the good news that Jesus has defeated sin, death, and evil through his own death and resurrection and is making all things new, even us. The gospel changes what we believe (doctrinal), who we are (personal), and where we live (missional).

Discussion Questions:
- *Is this different from what you used to think of when you heard the word gospel?*
- *Which way of looking at the gospel are you most familiar with?*
- *Of the three aspects, which one do you think you could grow in the most?*

Later this Week:

Get everyone together later in the week to walk or drive around your neighborhood and pray for it. You will be tempted to do this from the safety of your living room, but brave outside to pray as Steve Hawthorne says, "on site with insight." Split into groups and walk leisurely asking the Spirit to open your eyes and ears to images, issues, hopes, and dreams for your city.

Remember, to pray for the other churches and Christians in the city. Pray on site with insight.

- Who are the oppressed in our neighborhood?
- Who is not welcomed into the life of our neighborhood?
- Who is hungry, poor, marginalized, enslaved?
- What are the hidden or culturally acceptable idols of our neighborhood (materialism, isolation, abuse, and idolatry)?

WEEK 4:
Living the Gospel

Big Picture:
- Putting all we've learned about the gospel together.
- Our response to the gospel: repentance and faith.
- Reminding each other of the gospel.

Preparing to Lead:

This is the week you begin applying the gospel in community. This is where the gospel ceases to be something you agree with or can recite and something you live.

You will be establishing the pattern for how you will all grow up in the gospel: repentance and faith. Be certain the definitions are clear. Following this week you will begin implementing the practice and working towards discipleship groups (Fight Clubs, Triads, DNA groups) where men and women will walk with each other in fighting against sin and its lies and trusting Jesus and his promises.

Before the Discussion:

Have another leader share their story. Again, pray in response. This will be the last story shared until the end of the primer. Through the past three weeks, you have modeled honesty, repentance, faith, and doubt. You will want to create more space for other people's stories after the primer.

The Discussion:

The gospel empowers neither religion nor rebellion, but repentance and faith in Jesus Christ as Lord.

The Gospel is Not Religious Performance

What should motivate our obedience to God? Duty, feeling, or something else? Tim Keller has notes that religion says, "I obey, therefore I am accepted," but the gospel says, "I am accepted, therefore I obey." This is great news! It means we are motivated by God's acceptance of us in Christ, not to be accepted. The Scriptures appeal to gospel motivation. You don't have to perform for God or the church! You don't have to impress God because Jesus impressed God for you. You don't have to pretend to be perfect, because all of us are imperfect people clinging to a perfect Christ, being perfected by the Spirit!

The Gospel is Not Spiritual License

Does this mean we just obey when we feel accepted or when we sense the truth of the gospel? Should we keep on sinning so grace can abound even more? Paul says "by no means" (Romans 6:1-4). This is driving under our own spiritual license, not under grace. Spiritual license deceives us by saying: "Because God has forgiven me, I'm free to disobey." The truth of the gospel is: "Because God has forgiven me in Christ, I'm bound to obey." The gospel points us to Jesus as Christ and as Lord. The religious are bound to keeping rules, and the rebellious are bound to breaking rules. The gospel, however, tells us that we are bound, not to rules, but to Christ. We need to relentlessly remind one another of the beauty, sufficiency, and glory of Christ. He's worth every step of obedience, every act of holiness.

The gospel calls us to holiness, not legalism, and here is more good news. . . it is for our joy! There is true joy in learning to turn away from the sin that destroys us, and to turn to Jesus who is the Giver of life, joy, and peace.

Discussion Questions:

- *Do you lean more towards religious performance or spiritual license?*
- *Have you ever felt like you had to perform spiritually to be accepted by God?*

- *Have you ever found license, or rebellion unsatisfying?*

Responding to the Gospel: Repentance & Faith

When we consider what the gospel really is, and what it is not, how should we respond to it?

Key Text: *"Now after John was arrested, Jesus came into Galilee, proclaiming the gospel of God, and saying, 'The time is fulfilled, and the kingdom of God is at hand; repent and believe in the gospel.'"* —Mark 1:14-15

When Jesus preached the gospel he demanded a response—repent and believe.

Repentance

You may have heard the words "repent" and "believe" before, but what do they really mean? Many people hear "repent" and they think it means to say sorry, feel bad about sin, and ask God for forgiveness. Many people hear "believe" and they think it means to agree with the fact that Jesus died for their sins and rose again. Both of these definitions are incomplete at best.

Faith

When Jesus said "repent" he was saying to turn away not only from sin, but to turn from the lies that sin deceives us with, and to turn towards something truer and better, to turn to Jesus and his true promises. We are encouraged to "believe" in Jesus, to cling to his promises, to put our hope, trust, and faith in him.

Take the deceptive promise of pride, for example. Pride says: "Find and cherish compliments and then you will be confident." But the gospel says, "Instead of trusting in compliments for confidence, believe that your sufficiency comes from God in Christ." 2 Corinthians 3:4-6: "Such is the confidence that we have through Christ toward God. Not that we are sufficient in ourselves to claim anything as coming from us, but our sufficiency is from God, who has made us competent." The gospel says: "Your confidence comes, not from your sufficiency, but from God who has made you sufficient in Jesus." Faith in the person of Jesus, who he is and what he has accomplished for us, is true saving, changing faith.

Discussion Questions

- *What do you think about the idea that "repentance is good news"?*
- *How can we learn to turn away from sin and it's lies to Jesus and his promises?*
- *As a community, what would it look like to be people that consistently reminded one another of this good news?*
- *What would it look like to help one another turn from sin and lies to Jesus, his promises, and true joy?*

Later this Week:

Have a guys night/girls night. If your group has children, you can do a guys night in/girls night out. You will want to pick places and environments where you can really talk and share. As you do reflect on the questions that were left at the end of this week:

- As a group of girls/guys, what would it look like to be people that consistently reminded one another of this good news?
- What would it look like to help one another turn from sin and lies to Jesus, his promises, and true joy?

COMMUNITY

WEEK 5:
What is Community?

Big Picture:
- *The gospel of Jesus is the center of community.*
- *How we begin sharing life as a community.*
- *Reminding each other of the gospel.*

Preparing to Lead:

We're now moving forward from the gospel toward community. Hopefully, your community has begun to experience community as you've spent quality time together, shared some stories, and learned the gospel together.

This week is full. You may want to consider breaking it up among different leaders to guide the discussion just to help maintain the flow of conversation. One leader could teach on what is community and what isn't.

You will want to give plenty of time for these discussions because they usually go deep quickly. The questions are helpful in unearthing our preconceived notions of community and leading us towards true community.

Before the Discussion:
This is a packed week. You're just going to have to jump right in.

The Discussion:

Discussion Question: *What comes to mind when you hear the word "community"?*

Key Text: *"I hope to come to you soon, but I am writing these things to you so that, if I delay, you may know how one ought to behave in the household of God, which is the church of the living God, a pillar and buttress of the truth."* —1 Timothy 3:15

Paul uses a family metaphor to describe the church—"the household of God, which is the church of the living God." In fact, he opens almost every letter to churches by addressing them as "brothers and sisters." In the Bible, community is conceived of as family. This family is also called the church, which is created to support and protect the truth of the gospel (1 Timothy 2:4). Community, then, is a set of relationships centered on the gospel. The church is made alive by the Spirit to give and receive the gospel as God's new community. In short, community is a gospel-centered family.

What Community Isn't[1]
Community is not:

- *A Book Club—centered on "your doctrine" or curriculum or even the Bible.*
- *A Social Club—centered on "your connections" or your relational need.*
- *A Counseling Group—centered on "your therapy needs."*
- *A Social Service Group—centered on "your good deeds."*
- *A Neighborhood Association—centered on "your neighborhood and geography."*
- *An Affinity Group—centered on "your stage of life or preferences."*
- *An Event or Meeting—centered on a convenient time-slot.*

Discussion Questions:

- *Why do these things fail as good centers for community? For example, what happens to community when it is centered on your needs after your needs are met? What hap-*

---

[1] This list was inspired by our friends in the Soma Family of Churches: www.wearesoma.org.

pens when relationships get difficult and conflict comes when your community is centered on your relational needs?

- What is it about these things that makes them easy or tempting to place at the center of community?
- If community is not centered on these things, what do you think it should be centered on?
- If Christ is truly the center of the community, then how do you think the "centers" mentioned above can be addressed?

What Community Is

"And they devoted themselves to the apostles' teaching and the fellowship, to the breaking of bread and the prayers. And awe came upon every soul, and many wonders and signs were being done through the apostles. And all who believed were together and had all things in common. And they were selling their possessions and belongings and distributing the proceeds to all, as any had need. And day by day, attending the temple together and breaking bread in their homes, they received their food with glad and generous hearts, praising God and having favor with all the people. And the Lord added to their number day by day those who were being saved." —Acts 2:42-47

Discussion Questions:

- What are the striking elements of community in this description of the church?
- What is this community like? How would you describe the nature of the community (apart from its activity)?
- Why do you think they lived this way? (Look at Acts 2:37-41)
- What are they doing? (Make a list in your own words. This could include: praying, celebrating, learning, caring for one another, caring for the poor, commitment, sharing the gospel, sharing life, awe for what God is doing, generosity, people liking them, people observing their lives, sharing, meeting needs.)

- *Which of the activities listed in Acts 2 excite you?*
- *Which are challenging to your pre-conceived ideas of community?*
- *How often do you do these things as community vs. as an individual? (Prayer, worship, learning, caring for one another, sharing the gospel, etc).*

In this passage we see a glimpse of the early church, a community of people who were devoted not only to Jesus, but also to one another. They prayed together, and they ate together. They shared gospel teachings, and they shared their possessions! We see a beautiful picture of a community of people who were so devoted to the gospel that they were devoted to one another. They lived more like a tight family than a loose collection of individuals. They didn't "go" to church because they "were" the church.

What if we tried to recover this biblical pattern of community? What if we decided not to be a group of individuals who try to follow Jesus on our own, occasionally gathering for a church service or a bible study; rather, we committed to being a community of people devoted to Jesus and one another!

Discussion Question: *Do you find this kind of community attractive or intimidating? Why?*

The hope of the gospel is that we don't have to be a perfect community since Jesus was perfect for us. When we let one another down, we point to Jesus who lifts us up. The gospel, not religious rules, unites the church. Religious community, however, says: "If I keep the community rules, then people will accept me," but gospel community says: "We are already accepted in Christ; therefore, we love, forgive, and accept one another." This is great news! The gospel frees us from performing for God or for the church! You don't have to impress God because Jesus impressed God for you. You don't have to pretend to be perfect, because all of us are imperfect people clinging to a perfect Christ, being perfected by the Spirit!

Discussion Questions:

- *What would it look like for us to become this kind of community?*
- *What must change in our hearts?*
- *What must change in our daily-lives?*
- *What must change in how we view our lives?*
- *Is it worth it? Why?*

Later this Week:

Do something fun as a group. If you have kids in your group, cater it to something they might enjoy. Otherwise, plan something where your community can simply exist together in the city and where people can invite their friends to join. Could be a simple cook-out, concert in the park, trip to the zoo, or game night. Be creative. The *what* doesn't matter so much.

WEEK 6:
The Defeaters of Community

Big Picture:
- *Sharing life together. Practically inviting others into ours and joining people in theirs.*
- *What a missional community does. What are the "activities" of a missional community?*
- *Why and how people say "no" to community.*

Preparing to Lead:
This is another full discussion and very much a rubber meets the road moment for every community. This week people will begin deciding how seriously they want to take this endeavor. The theory begins to fade into the background as the reality sets in: this will cost me my whole life.

The feel of this week will be like a very important family meeting, where you decide to commit to being a community instead of individuals. Will your community open your lives up? It definitely requires sacrifices, but it is definitely worth it. You are inviting people to nothing short of following Jesus. There isn't a better way to spend a life.

Before the Discussion:
This is a packed week. You're just going to have to jump right in, again.

The Discussion:
Last week, we spent time discussing what community is and isn't. We discussed what the center truly is and what it looks

like to open our lives to gospel-centered community. But, what does gospel-centered community *really* look like?

Ordinary Life: Making Your Life A Communal Life
We certainly can't be family with one another if we settle for just being together once a week, but we also live busy lives with many commitments. Many of us have many responsibilities with our jobs, school, families, hobbies, and the ordinary demands of everyday life (laundry, cleaning, cooking).

You are probably wondering: "Am I too busy for this?" or "Am I ready for this sort of thing?" You may be asking: "Is being the church going to make me busier than I already am?" How do we find time to be together more than once a week?

Remember, church isn't something you attend; it's something that you are! You are the church as you work, go to school, participate in sports, enjoy hobbies, and do ordinary things. Do ordinary things but with gospel intentionality. In other words, do the everyday things of life, but do them in a way that shows your devotion to Jesus, one another, and your neighbors and city! We encourage one another to do things you already do, but to do them with others in community.

Think through your average week, *what are some of your commitments and weekly rhythms? (Below is a list to get you started)*
- **Chores:** Yard-work, home improvement, auto care, etc.
- **Errands:** Grocery shopping and going to the bank.
- **Recreation:** Vacations, hobbies, exercise, sports leagues, book clubs, etc.
- **Meals:** Most people eat twenty-one meals a week. You could share some.
- **Service:** Instead of everyone volunteering at separate good causes, you could all serve the same one. Even within your local church, you could all commit to serving in the same area together.

Discussion Questions:

- *What would it take to include others in these things? Think both spiritually (have to show need) and practically (have to communicate/plan).*
- *What sacrifices would have to be made to line up our lives? Change sports teams? Change gym memberships?*
- *What are some ways we could grow in living out these areas of life together?*

Reality Check: Community doesn't line up with the Ideal

Don't get me wrong, the picture of community we've been discussing is a beautiful one, but in real life it's messy. There is a problem with community—it's full of people, people who sin. We will inevitably snub, gossip, disregard, and complain about one another. It's an imperfect community.

To enter into true community, our ideal community must be surrendered. We need to recognize several things about gospel-centered community. First, conflict and tension in relationships do not take God by surprise; in fact, he appoints it as a grace for our Christlike change (James 1; Romans 8; Colossians 3)! Second, imperfect community also creates the opportunity to give and receive the gospel of grace by forgiving and forbearing with one another. Because God extends forgiveness and grace to us, we can extend grace and forgiveness to one another (Ephesians 4:32). Third, the mess of community helps us become a maturing community that speaks the truth in love to one another (Ephesians 4:15). This is good news because we all need love, and we all need truth! As we mature, we learn how to remind one another of God's love and his truth in our everyday.

Discussion Questions:

- *How can conflict and tension in relationships be used by God to change you?*
- *What is hard about forgiving others who let you down or sinned against you?*

- *What are your expectations from other people in this community?*
- *What would it look like to be a community that deals with conflict with the gospel?*
- *What would it look like to speak the truth in love to one another?*

Later This Week:

This week, encourage everyone to take some time alone or as families to rest. Ask them to reflect on their lives: what are the costs and blessings of following Jesus, because it will always include community?

Also, challenge each person and family in the community to share a meal with a neighbor or co-worker. Give them the assignment of simply listening to them.

MISSION

WEEK 7:
The Mission of a "Missional Community"

Big Picture:
- Defining and understanding the mission of community.
- Defining and understanding discipleship/evangelism.

Preparing to Lead:

You're turning another page in your community's progression through this primer. You're developing habits and relationships that are normalizing. Hopefully, your community is growing in unity, love, and faith. Congratulations!

This week you will be redefining old topics about mission, discipleship, and evangelism. It is important to shed light on preconceived ideas and learn afresh what God's mission is, and what it means to be a disciple.

Following the discussion you will spend time together in prayer. So, you will want to keep an eye on the clock to leave you with at least 30 minutes of time to pray.

The Discussion:

Discussion Question: *What comes to mind when you hear the word "mission"?*

> *"And Jesus came and said to them, 'All authority in heaven and on earth has been given to me. Go therefore and make disciples of all nations, baptizing them in the name of the Father and of the Son and of the Holy Spirit, teaching them to observe all that I have commanded you. And behold, I am with you always, to the end of the age.'" —Matthew 28:18-20*

Parting words are a big deal. In Matthew we get to over-hear Jesus' parting words to his disciples, who were the beginning of the first "missional community."

When we say "mission" many things may come to mind: a trip to Africa, or a day of work at a soup kitchen, or even mentoring students at a low-income apartment community. All those are great things to do and can be a great way to "show and share the gospel," but ultimately the mission of the first disciples was to make more disciples of Jesus. Mission is another word for purpose, as in life purpose. Here, Jesus gives his disciples the life-long purpose of making disciples of Jesus. It isn't a side job or a hobby, but an all encompassing orientation for life. As a disciple, you are called to make disciples.

Redefining Discipleship
Question: *What do you think discipleship means?*

When we say our mission is to "make disciples" most people think of two things: winning people over to Jesus (evangelism) or helping a follower of Jesus learn to obey him (discipleship). But when we look at Mathew 28, we don't see an either/or discipleship; in fact we see both "evangelism" and "discipleship."

"Go therefore and make disciples of all nations, baptizing them in the name of the Father and of the Son and of the Holy Spirit."

Looks like "evangelism"...

"Teaching them to observe everything I have commanded you"

Looks like "discipleship"...

The Great Commission is neither evangelism- nor discipleship-centered. It is gospel-centered. The command to make disciples is described three ways: 1) being sent in the power of Jesus, 2) baptizing into the name of Jesus, and 3) teaching the commands of Jesus. The mission of the church is radically Jesus-centered!

If the gospel is truly at the center of the church and her mission, then both discipleship and evangelism will reflect this focus on Jesus Christ. Belief in Jesus changes what we believe, who we are, and where we live. We will go, baptize, and teach Jesus wherever we live.

The most succinct statement of the gospel is: "Jesus Christ is Lord." Disciples of Jesus are committed to sharing and showing that "Jesus is Lord" in every area of life and in every domain of society: work, family, government, education, entertainment, and all of culture. Therefore, we aim to make disciples of Jesus who do the same: disciples who make great culture, redeem social ill, and share the whole gospel!

Discussion Question:

- *How does this description of discipleship change or challenge your perspective on mission?*
- *What are your fears or concerns about making disciples?*
- *How are you growing as a disciple of Jesus?*
- *How would making disciples in a community enhance your mission?*

After the Discussion:

Pray for one another and your neighborhood. Use the list or observations from your walk around your neighborhood a few weeks ago to guide your time of prayer. Pray for your hearts to be concerned and gracious towards the people around you. Pray for God's guidance in leading your community in caring for and loving the people God has place around you. Confess how Jesus is not Lord and pray for renewed submission to Jesus.

Later This Week:

Have a picnic, party, or grill-out where you invite everyone—co-workers, friends, neighbors, etc. Encourage everyone to be active as "hosts" regardless of where it is, engaging people and introducing them to each other. Give everyone the task of listening and hearing the stories of the people who come. If you are new to a city or neighborhood, make invitations and deliver them to people in your neighborhood.

WEEK 8:
Being on Mission Together

Big Picture:
- God and mission.
- What it means to be "sent" and how a missional community is a sent.
- Thinking about those you are "sent to."

Preparing to Lead:

This is a long discussion as it wraps up the primer and brings into focus the mission. Your goals are to ensure that the community has a grasp on the why of a missional community, that it isn't a fad but born out of God's identity and sending. Also, that your community views themselves as sent by God.

Lastly, you will focus on who you are sent to. You may not have time to unpack and discern who God is calling you to. However, you will want to introduce it and pick up where you left off next week as you pursue a unified and shared mission. Some people know exactly who they are sent to. If this is the case begin answering the questions. If your community doesn't have a shared mission, create a plan or process together for how you will discover that. Hint: prayer and engagement with others is part of this process.

The Discussion:

A Sending God

God is missional. The *missio dei* is a Latin phrase that classically refers to God's "mission" or "sending"—the Father sending the Son, and the Father and Son sending the Spirit. As a missional

God, the Father, Son, and Spirit, create and send a missional people and churches.

- The Father sent the Son
- The Father and the Son sent the Spirit
- The Father, Son, and Spirit send the Church

A Missional Community

The result of the church being sent is that we live as a community of disciples who are not only devoted to Jesus and to one another, but are also devoted to our neighbors and our city. When we come to Christ, we are sent on his mission.

Mission is not an option for followers of Jesus, or something reserved for "super-spiritual or radical Christians"; mission is for everybody! The mission of making disciples who make good culture, redeem social ill, and share a whole gospel is the joy and responsibility of every Christian.

A missional community, then, is a group of people who are devoted to Jesus, to one another, and to their neighbors and city! They are disciples of Jesus who are committed to making more disciples of Jesus! Therefore, mission is not merely a monthly trip to feed the homeless or a trip to Africa to serve in an orphanage (although those are great things to do!). Mission is something that happens in our everyday lives as we follow Jesus. Mission is not merely an activity; it is our identity!

Being missional is being yourself. It is making disciples where you live with your community as you collectively follow Jesus.

Discussion Question: *How we need to grow in order to embrace Jesus' call to mission?*

Sent Like Jesus

"Jesus said to them again, 'Peace be with you. As the Father has sent me, even so I am sending you.'" —John 20:21

If the way the Father sent Jesus is the way that Jesus sends us, then it is important to ask: "How did the Father send Jesus?"

The answer to that question is shocking!

God sent Jesus to become human! The God of the universe became a man, experienced hunger, thirst, pain, and betrayal. He lived among us, as one of us. Notice God didn't ask people to come to him; he went to people.

Most of us have experienced the opposite when it comes to "church." The church builds buildings, plans services, and asks people to "come to church." Jesus sends the church.

If we are to be sent like Jesus, then we should stop expecting people to come to church, and we should start taking church to people! After all, the church is not a building or a service; it is the people of God on the mission of Christ. The Church is us. We must go with one another into our neighborhoods, places of employment, kids' schools, and favorite hangouts to make disciples.

Discussion Question: *How might this change the way you approach non-Christians?*

Mission is for Everybody (And Happens in the Everyday)
"And he gave the apostles, the prophets, the evangelists, the shepherds and teachers, to equip the saints for the work of ministry, for building up the body of Christ." —Ephesians 4:11-12

There is no such thing as a spectator Christian; we are all in this together! God didn't give these five leaders to the church in order for them to do missional community. Rather, he gave them as gifts to equip everyday people for missional community.

Where can you begin? Look around! You live next to people, work with people, and are friends with people who do not know Jesus.

Mission happens in the everyday things of life: backyard grill-outs with the neighbors, lunch breaks with your co-workers, attending concerts, watching films, play dates, and happy hours. The missional church is not about adding activities to an already busy life; rather, it is a matter of being yourself in the everyday with gospel intentionality.

- *How can you begin to live your normal life with greater gospel intentionality?*

- *Who can you begin to disciple to Jesus?*

Let's Get Specific

If being "sent" is part of our identity, then it would be a good idea to know who we are sent to. A great starting place is your group of friends, the people who live in your neighborhood, apartment complex, or dorm room, your co-workers, people you share a passion or hobby with, or the other regulars at your favorite hangout.

If we are going to know how the gospel is "good news" for the people we are sent to, we also need to know them! Here are five questions to help you get specific about discipling others with the gospel.

1. **People:** What people is God sending you to? Where do they live and hang out? How could we reorient our lives to be with them?
2. **Language:** What "language" do they speak? Are these people young families, business professionals, hipsters, etc?
3. **Value:** What is most important to them? Success, money, relationships, independence, etc?
4. **Gospel:** How is the gospel good news to them? How does it address their values? How is the gospel better than what they value most right now?
5. **Needs:** What are their needs? How does Jesus meet those needs? How can we be a part of meeting their needs in a way that "shows" the gospel?

Later This Week:

Have everyone take some time to work through these questions for your identified mission as a missional community.

Come back to these questions regularly. We should never stop asking them so we can meaningfully communicate the gospel to others and make disciples of Jesus.

MOVING FORWARD:
Missional Commitments

Following eight weeks of learning and experimenting with missional community, you may want to create a missional commitment or what some call a covenant. This commitment is to God, one another, and your city. Why would you want to create one? What is it? And what should you include in one as you lead your community, shepherd your people through this process?

Why Make Missional Commitments?

The purpose of this guide, as stated up front, is that we would move from theory to practice, from the classroom to the city, and from talking about "missional community" deeper into being a missional community. James says it this way, "Be doers of the word, not hearers only" (James 1:22).

Many of us are convinced that missional communities are the way to be the church, to really be devoted to Jesus, one another, and our neighbors and city. We also realize that this doesn't come easy as we rub up against our own sin, individualism, consumerism, as well as anything else we may be trying to unlearn from "church experience."

If we "hear" missional community but don't "do" missional community, with a clear sense of how it applies to our everyday lives, we'll be like the person who looks in the mirror but forgets who he or she is. We want you and others to be "blessed in your doing," which is why we want to make a missional commitment.

A COUPLE DISCLAIMERS:

1) We will fail

We won't perfectly live out what we commit to, we never do. The good news is that when we fail in loving one another and our neighbors, we have the gospel through which God freely forgives us! We don't "do missional community" to earn Gods favor; rather, in Christ we have God's favor to be a missional community, imperfections and all!

This commitment will not serve as a legalistic document to judge one another's performance; rather, it will be something we can revisit every once in a while to see how we are progressing in living out our devotion to Jesus, one another, and our neighbors and city.

2) This is not an "in" or "out"

Some people sit through these discussions but are not ready to make a missional commitment, that's okay. Although we want everyone to be challenged and encouraged to be a faithful disciple of Jesus, we are not here to twist arms. We're glad everyone is here.

In fact, encourage those who don't want to make a commitment to continue being part of your missional community. Let them know: "We want you with us." The Missional Commitment is not intended to create an "in or out" dynamic, but rather, to clarify a common commitment to being a community that lives out what we believe in everyday life. This commitment will help shape a core of committed people that will benefit our whole community and city.

By God's Grace We Will Grow in Our Devotion to Christ by _____.

In this first section, we want to come up with ways we will practically grow in our devotion to Jesus this year.

Some groups may commit to reading the Gospels together, attending Sunday gatherings to hear the gospel, discussing sermons over a meal on a weeknight, starting fight clubs or initiating 1-1 discipleship times. Others may commit to developing their prayer life, memorizing scripture, attending a conference together, or reading books on gospel marriage or parenting.

This section may include a commitment to Christ-centered study of the Scriptures in discipleship groups, sermon discussions, memorizing Scripture together, inviting counsel from the community on a whole range of personal issues, doing a personal change project in community (see Tim Chester's *You Can Change*), and much more. You may want to cultivate better listening skills in Spirit-led decision-making or devoting entire nights to prayer for one another and the city.

The idea is that you, as a community, answer these questions yourself. Be honest about where you need to grow in your devotion to Jesus this year, and be creative and faithful with how you plan to do that. Get honest and get specific!

By God's Grace We Will Grow in Our Devotion to One Another by _____.

This should be fun as you look around at one another and ask: "How would we treat one another differently if we are family?" Since you are family in Christ, why not live like it?!

In this section you may commit to share more meals, help one another in employment search, help one another financially, with childcare, with transportation, and the list goes on and on.

It may also include a commitment to sharing in the rhythms of church life: Celebrate (and Suffer), Eat, Recreate, Listen, and Serve. Here you can get real specific on how you can grow in sharing these rhythms.

This is exciting because no two groups are the same. There are unique ways in which your community can be devoted to one another, and this is where you get to commit to those things!

By God's Grace We Will Grow in Our Devotion to Our Neighbors and City by _____.

Here is where you get to think like a missionary, you get to look around, pray, and ask God to show you who he is calling you to make disciples of.

Don't just stop at identifying your mission, but get specific on a plan to engage the mission. How can you orient your lives to spend time with the people you are called to? How is the gospel good news to those people?

Some groups may be called to a specific neighborhood or apartment community. Other groups may be called to make disciples among a specific people group (i.e. Artists on the Eastside, downtown urban professionals, the neglected kids of a housing project.) Other groups may feel called to make disciples among the homeless, the working poor, or refugees.

Try to get specific, realizing that the Lord may not call everyone into the same mission. Take time to recognize the mission field of vocation and discuss how you can support one another in that. However, don't just state a generic mission. We have found that the more broad the mission, the less traction it gets.

We Will Count the Cost of Being a Missional Community

Following Jesus will cost you something, and that is actually good news in the Kingdom of God as it is more blessed to give than receive! We often see that as a result of God's grace everyday people begin to be radically generous with their time, their creativity, and their finances.

It is important to "count the cost" in making a Missional Commitment, and to get specific on how you plan to give. Some good questions to ask are:

- How can I be generous with my time?
- How can I be generous with my creativity?
- How can I be generous financially to see the gospel go forward in our community, our church, our city, and beyond!

By God's Grace, We Commit to the Process of Becoming a Missional Community.

Since Jesus Christ is the head of the church and the center of our community, he should be our primary focus. Every issue in our life has an answer in Christ. As a community, we have the wonderful privilege of joining together to explore, through the ups and downs, how Christ is central and meaningful.

In this section you are committing to being a community that "speaks the truth in love" to one another. You are committing to be a confessing, counseling, repenting community, which continually reorients one another to Christ and his promises.

Example of a Missional Commitment

Allandale/Crestview Missional Community

By Gods grace we are a missional community in the Allandale/Crestview neighborhood. Because of the gospel of Jesus we want to grow in our devotion to him, to one another, and to our neighbors and city.

Devotion to Jesus

By Gods grace we commit to growing in our devotion to Jesus by:

- Gathering with the other MCs on Sundays for worship and gospel teaching.
- Gathering on Tuesday evenings for dinner, discussion, and prayer focused on the gospel. (X will organize meal/childcare schedule, X will lead discussion, X will write down and send out prayer requests).
- Read Paul E. Miller's *The Praying Life* together and discuss.
- Starting "Discipleship Groups" that meet monthly to promote gospel-centered spiritual growth.
- Attending a Parenting Seminar together.

Devotion to One Another

By Gods grace we commit to growing in our devotion to one another by:

- Committing to regularly pray for, encourage, and forgive one another.
- Establishing an "emergency fund" (overseen by two capable leaders) so that we can help any of us who is unexpectedly in a financial crisis.
- Having a monthly "Sunday Night Family Dinner" together. Also, open to friends and neighbors. (Organized by X).
- Weekend summer vacation together (tentative)—providing childcare for one another when there is need.
- The men in our group will regularly check on single mom to see how we can help her as a single mother.(i.e. yard work, heavy lifting, etc).
- Faithfully encourage X through his battle with cancer through prayer, regular visits, and providing meals via a care calendar.

Devotion to Our Neighbor and City

By Gods grace we commit to growing in our devotion to our neighbors and city by:

- We feel we have been sent to the Allandale/Crestview neighborhoods, in particular, the people we regularly interact with in our neighborhoods, Gullet Elementary, and Lamar Middle School.
- We plan to regularly be present and to serve at the local schools: specifically painting the parent resource room at Lamar Middle School, volunteering at the LamarFest, sponsoring the end of year sports banquet, and pursuing other opportunities to serve the community. X will organize the serve opportunities with the schools since they have kids attending.
- We will regularly pray as a group for our neighbors and friends who do not know and believe the good news of Jesus.
- We will host bi-monthly parties that we intentionally invite our neighbors to.
- We will serve regularly with X as a way of serving the working poor and single parent families in Wooten

Park, and inviting our neighbors to serve with us so they can see the gospel expressed in love for the poor.

- We will pray for (and train for) a new MC to be formed and sent out of ours to either Crestview, Wooten Park, Northwest Hills, or Hyde Park/Rosedale area.

APPENDIX I:
Weekly Handouts

Week 1: The Gospel is Doctrinal

The gospel is the good news that Jesus has defeated sin, death, and evil through his own death and resurrection and is making all things new, even us.

This definition of the gospel can be broken down into three aspects.

1. The gospel is *doctrinal*: it changes what we believe.
2. The gospel is *personal*: it changes who we are.
3. The gospel is *missional*: it changes where and how we live.

The Gospel is Doctrinal: It Changes What We Believe

Key Text: *"Now I would remind you, brothers, of the gospel I preached to you, which you received, in which you stand, and by which you are being saved, if you hold fast to the word I preached to you—unless you believed in vain. For I delivered to you as of first importance what I also received: that Christ died for our sins in accordance with the Scriptures, that he was buried, that he was raised on the third day in accordance with the Scriptures, and that he appeared to Cephas, then to the twelve."* —1 Corinthians 15:1-5

Personal Reflection

The Bible is the best place to begin to understand the message of the gospel. Read the following passages and write down 2-3 key points that summarize that passage. Don't be surprised if the same key points continue to emerge!

- John 3:16-17
- Romans 3:23
- Ephesians 2:8-10
- Romans 1:16
- Galatians 1:8
- 1 Peter 1:12

Now in one to three sentences, using your own words, answer the question: *What is the gospel?*

Week 2: The Gospel is Personal

The gospel is the good news that Jesus has defeated sin, death, and evil through his own death and resurrection and is making all things new, even us.

Beholding Jesus

The gospel changes us into the image and likeness of Jesus. The gospel frees us to admit our failures, because our worth doesn't hang on our success. Rather, our worth hangs on Jesus' success, his life over death.

> *"And we all, with unveiled face, beholding the glory of the Lord, are being transformed into the same image from one degree of glory to another. For this comes from the Lord who is the Spirit." —2 Corinthians 3:18*

Becoming Like Jesus

The gospel changes who we are by changing what we look at! The gospel offers hope because it gives us the eyes to behold Jesus as well as the power to become like him. The power for gospel change is the person of the Holy Spirit.

> *"Beholding the glory of the Lord, are being transformed into the same image from one degree of glory to another. For this comes from the Lord who is the Spirit" —2 Corinthians 3:17-18*

Personal Reflection

Using the Scriptures above, think through and wrestle with these questions in your own life.

- Do you want to change? Why? What causes you to change?
- Where do you look for success? How do you hide your failures?
- What is the gospel in the face of your success, failure, and power to change?

Week 3: The Gospel is Missional

The gospel is the good news that Jesus has defeated sin, death, and evil through his own death and resurrection and is making all things new, even us.

The Gospel Changes Where You Live

"The Spirit of the Lord is upon me, because he has anointed me to proclaim good news to the poor. He has sent me to proclaim liberty to the captives and recovering of sight to the blind, to set at liberty those who are oppressed, to proclaim the year of the Lord's favor." —Luke 4:18-19, Isaiah 61

The gospel changes everything. It is not only good news for us, but also for our neighbors, the poor, our city, and the world. It affects the social, cultural, and physical fabric of the universe.

The Church Joins the Mission

Because the gospel changes what we believe and who we are, it should change where we live. We should make great culture, redeem social ill, and share a whole gospel. Christians should be among the most creative, neighborly, compassionate people in the city. If the gospel truly affects everything, then it should affect everything in our lives. It should change where we live.

Personal Reflection

Read and reflect on these passages and take notes on what God is changing and who Christians are in this recreation.

- Matthew 28:18-20
- 2 Corinthians 5:17-20
- Isaiah 61:4
- Revelation 21

We've now unpacked the three aspects of the gospel: doctrinal, personal, and missional. Which way of looking at the gospel are you most familiar with? Of the three aspects, which one do you think you could grow in the most?

Week 4: Responding to the Gospel

The gospel empowers neither religion nor rebellion, but repentance and faith in Jesus Christ as Lord.

The Gospel is *Not* Religious Performance or Spiritual License!

The religious are bound to keeping rules, and the rebellious are bound to breaking rules. The gospel, however, tells us that we are bound, not to rules, but to Christ.

Repentance & Faith

> *"Now after John was arrested, Jesus came into Galilee, proclaiming the gospel of God, and saying, 'The time is fulfilled, and the kingdom of God is at hand; repent and believe in the gospel.'" —Mark 1:14-15*

When Jesus said "repent" he was saying to turn away not only from sin, but to turn from the lies that sin deceives us with, and to turn towards something truer and better, to turn to Jesus. We are encouraged to "believe" in Jesus, to cling to his promises, to put our hope, trust, and faith in him.

Personal Reflection

- *Where do you look for hope, satisfaction, peace, approval, power, and comfort apart from Jesus?*
- *How good are those things in giving you what they promised?*
- *What does Jesus promise in the gospel?*
- *What would it look like to not only stop sinning, but start believing in the gospel of Jesus?*

Week 5: What Is Community?

"I hope to come to you soon, but I am writing these things to you so that, if I delay, you may know how one ought to behave in the household of God, which is the church of the living God, a pillar and buttress of the truth." —1 Timothy 3:15

What Community Isn't
- A Book Club
- A Social Club
- A Counseling Group
- A Social Service Group
- A Neighborhood Association
- An Affinity Group
- A Dinner Party
- An Event or Meeting

What Community Is
"And they devoted themselves to the apostles' teaching and the fellowship, to the breaking of bread and the prayers. And awe came upon every soul, and many wonders and signs were being done through the apostles. And all who believed were together and had all things in common. And they were selling their possessions and belongings and distributing the proceeds to all, as any had need. And day by day, attending the temple together and breaking bread in their homes, they received their food with glad and generous hearts, praising God and having favor with all the people. And the Lord added to their number day by day those who were being saved." —Acts 2:42-47

Personal Reflection
Using the passage above, make two lists. In one list, write about the nature, quality, and essence of this community. In the other, write what the community does and their actions.

- *What would it look like for you to become this kind of community?*

- *What must change in you hearts? How you view your life?*

Week 6: The Defeaters of Community

Church isn't something you attend; it's something that you are! You are the church as you work, go to school, participate in sports, enjoy hobbies, and do ordinary things. So, do ordinary things but with gospel intentionality. In other words, do the everyday things of life, but do them in a way that shows your devotion to Jesus, one another, and your neighbors and city!

Ordinary Life: Making Your Life A Communal Life

Think through your average week, *what are some of your commitments and weekly rhythms?*

Community Doesn't Look Like The Ideal But Is Messy

1. Conflict in relationships does not take God by surprise. He appoints it as a grace for our Christlike change (James 1, Romans 8, Colossians 3).
2. Imperfect community creates the opportunity to give and receive the gospel of grace by forgiving and forbearing with one another. (Ephesians 4:32).
3. The mess of community helps us become a maturing community that speaks the truth in love to one another (Ephesians 4:15).

Personal Reflection:

- *Do you ever find yourself "too busy" to be the church?*
- *What happens when parents are too busy to be family to their kids?*
- *Why are you so busy?*
- *What is so important that it draws you away from your family?*
- *What unspoken ideals and expectations do you have for community?*
- *What if your community was filled with conflict and mess?*
- *How would that teach you the gospel?*

Week 7: The Mission of a "Missional Community"

"And Jesus came and said to them, 'All authority in heaven and on earth has been given to me. Go therefore and make disciples of all nations, baptizing them in the name of the Father and of the Son and of the Holy Spirit, teaching them to observe all that I have commanded you. And behold, I am with you always, to the end of the age.'" —Matthew 28:18-20

When we say our mission is to "make disciples" most people think of two things: winning people over to Jesus (evangelism) or helping a follower of Jesus learn to obey him (discipleship). But when we look at Mathew 28, we don't see an either/or discipleship; in fact we see both "evangelism" and "discipleship."

The Great Commission is neither evangelism- nor discipleship-centered. It is gospel-centered. The command to make disciples is described three ways: 1) being sent in the power of Jesus, 2) baptizing into the name of Jesus, and 3) teaching the commands of Jesus. The mission of the church is radically Jesus-centered!

Personal Reflection

- *How does this description of discipleship change or challenge your perspective on mission?*
- *How are you making disciples? How are you growing as a disciple of Jesus?*
- *How would living in a community enhance your participation in the mission?*

Week 8: Being on Mission Together

A Sending God

God is missional. The *missio dei* is a Latin phrase that classically refers to God's "mission" or "sending"—the Father sending the Son, and the Father and Son sending the Spirit. As a missional God, the Father, Son, and Spirit, create and send a missional people and churches.

- The Father sent the Son
- The Father and the Son sent the Spirit
- The Father, Son, and Spirit send the Church

A Missional Community

A missional community, then, is a group of people who are devoted to Jesus, to one another, and to their neighbors and city! They are disciples of Jesus who are committed to making more disciples of Jesus!

Sent Like Jesus

"Jesus said to them again, 'Peace be with you. As the Father has sent me, even so I am sending you.'" —John 20:21

If the way the Father sent Jesus is the way that Jesus sends us, then it is important to ask: "How did the Father send Jesus?"

Mission is for Everybody

"And he gave the apostles, the prophets, the evangelists, the shepherds and teachers, to equip the saints for the work of ministry, for building up the body of Christ." —Ephesians 4:11-12

Mission happens in the everyday things of life: backyard grill-outs with the neighbors, lunch breaks with your co-workers, attending concerts, watching films, play dates, and happy hours. The missional church is not about adding activities to an already busy life; rather, it is a matter of being yourself in the everyday with gospel intentionality.

Personal Reflection

If being "sent" is part of our identity, then it would be a good idea to know who we are sent to. A great starting place is your group of friends, the people who live in your neighborhood, apartment complex, or dorm room; your co-workers, people you share a passion or hobby with, or the other regulars at your favorite hangout.

If we are going to know how the gospel is "good news" for the people we are sent to, we also need to know them! Here are five questions to help you get specific about discipling others with the gospel:

1. **People:** What people is God sending you to? Where do they live and hang out? How could we reorient our lives to be with them?
2. **Language:** What "language" do they speak? Are these people young families, business professionals, hipsters, etc?
3. **Value:** What is most important to them? Success, money, relationships, independence, etc?
4. **Gospel:** How is the gospel good news to them? How does it address their values? How is the gospel better than what they value most right now?
5. **Needs:** What are their needs? How does Jesus meet those needs? How can we be a part of meeting their needs in a way that "shows" the gospel?

APPENDIX II:
Leadership Role Description

Qualifications for Leaders

- **Motivated by the gospel.** It seems like a given, but many leaders can lead for other reasons.
- **Have a desire to help others grow in faith and obedience by pointing them to Jesus.**
- **Committed to the long process of helping others grow in faith and obedience.** It will take time and will not feel great or exciting most of the time.
- **Prayerful and dependent on God.** The Holy Spirit dwells within you. He is your helper that empowers you to love others. Leaders are those who pray and listen to the Spirit.
- **Servants to Jesus as Lord.** You are not building your resumé or gaining God's approval by leading a community. Instead, you are selflessly serving Jesus.
- **Honest about their own mess as they repent and believe the gospel.** Leaders who are honest and open about their struggles to believe the gospel.
- **Understands they can't make people change.** Leaders are faithful in sharing the gospel and trying new things, they are also quick to turn to God in prayer.

Posture of a Leader

The leaders of a missional community are examples of repentant and believing people. Being an example has often been the mark of a leader in Christian circles. However, the example being displayed is one of perfection. Someone with all the answers, free from sin and harmful vices, has the Bible memorized, and always knows the right thing to do. This, however, is a picture of Jesus, not leaders within a community or church. Instead, the example and model we find within the Bible is that the best leaders are humble, repentant, dependent on God, boast in nothing except God's grace in light of their sin, and servants.

What a Leader Does

As a leader, you will point people to the gospel in the Bible, speak the gospel in your own words, connect the gospel to people's stories, pray in light of the gospel, and call people to serve as demonstrations of the gospel. Leaders create an environment where community can happen.

- Prayer for each individual in your community.
- Regularly ask how your people are doing as individuals and families? How are you all doing together?
- Regularly ask what does it look like for our community to walk in repentance and faith? What does obedience look like for us? What is God calling us to?

APPENDIX III:
Leadership Development Plan

Picture of Health

Get with your co-leaders and leaders in training to think through this first section together.

A Missional Community exists because of the gospel. We are growing up into a deeper understanding and application of the gospel. We are taking the gospel to the neighborhood, city, and world through intentional missional engagement.

1. What would your Missional Community look like if it was thriving?

2. What would your neighborhood look like if it knew Jesus? What If they saw the transformation Jesus brings to a community of people?

3. What would you like to see happen this year in your MC?

4. What are goals that would move your community to take a few steps forward toward your MC vision?

Leading a Missional Community

In light of those hopes, dreams, and goals, use this section to explore what your role is in leading this missional community.

5. What is your role in leading your MC?

6. What areas do you feel like you need to grow in to lead your community?

Personal Development

Leaders are examples in communities of people who are walking in repentance and faith. They are growing in their knowledge of the gospel, believe in the gospel, and obedience to the gospel. One helpful way to think about this transformation is in terms of our head, heart, and hands being conformed to the image of Christ. As you work through this section, look for themes and connections across each area.

Head: Growing in Knowledge

"And do not be conformed to this world, but be transformed by the renewing of your mind, so that you may prove what the will of God is, that which is good and acceptable and perfect." —Romans 12:2

7. Where do you need to grow in knowledge? Are there things you need to know? Is there an issue you need to press into, an issue of Scripture to grow in deeper understanding of? Are there pieces of theology you need to learn? Are there aspects of gospel communities on mission that you still need to know?

8. How will you learn? (i.e. Is there a book or article to read, equipping session you need to attend, commentaries or studies to do, scripture to memorize, etc.?)

Heart: Growing in Belief

"I pray that the eyes of your heart may be enlightened, so that you will know what is the hope of His calling, what are the riches of the glory of His inheritance in the saints." —Ephesians 1:18

9. What areas of life do you need to grow in belief in the gospel? What areas do you need to see repentance in? What bondage are you volunteering for in your heart? What forgiveness needs to happen?

10. How will you grow in belief? (i.e. Shepherding conversations to have, questions and issues to bring up in discipleship and accountability groups, what material do you need to walk through, Redemption Immersion, prayer, fasting, retreats, etc.?)

Hands: Growing in Obedience, Skill, Practice.
"Teaching them to obey everything I have commanded." —Matthew 28:20

"Being no hearer who forgets but a doer who acts." —James 1:22-25

"Jesus glorified the Father by accomplishing the work he gave him to do." —John 17:4

11. What skills do you need practice in? Where are you excelling and need to keep growing at? Where are you failing to live what you believe? What skills do you need to develop? What things is God calling you to that you need to step into in obedience?

12. How will you grow in obedience, skill, and practice? (i.e. Are there trainings to attend, do you need to shadow someone, do you need to make a schedule, schedule some specific coaching to help you, are there opportunities for practice and feedback you need to pursue?)

ABOUT THE AUTHORS

Jonathan K. Dodson (MDiv; ThM, Gordon-Conwell Theological Seminary) serves as a pastor of City Life Church in Austin, Texas. He has written articles in numerous blogs and journals such as The Resurgence, The Journal of Biblical Counseling, and Boundless. He is author of *Gospel-Centered Discipleship*, *Raised?*, and *The Unbelievable Gospel* (Zondervan, 2014).

Brad Watson serves as a pastor at Bread & Wine Communities in Portland, OR. He lives in inner Southeast Portland with his wife, Mirela, and his daughter, Norah and co-author of *Raised? Finding Jesus by Doubting the Resurrection.*

OTHER GCD RESOURCES

Visit GCDiscipleship.com

Make, Mature, Multiply aims to help you become a disciple who truly understands the full joy of following Jesus. With a wide range of chapters from some of today's most battle-tested disciple-makers, this book is designed for any Christian seeking to know more about being a fully-formed disciple of Jesus who makes, matures, and multiplies fully-formed disciples of Jesus.

"*everPresent* does something that most books don't achieve in today's theological landscape. Most focus either on who God is or what we should do. Jeremy's efforts start with who God is to walk the reader down the path of what God has done, who we are because of God, and then, logically and succinctly, points us to naturally understand what we are to do because of this. I highly recommend picking this book up to better understand both the why and how of the life of those that follow Jesus."

SETH MCBEE
Executive Team Member, GCM Collective

"Luma Simms remembers vividly what it was like to be simply going through the motions of a spiritual life. She writes like someone who has just been awakened from a nightmare and can still describe it in detail. Luma's voice communicates the pain of forgetting what matters most, and may be just the voice to reach the half-awake."

FRED SANDERS
Associate Professor of Theology,
Torrey Honors Institute, Biola University

"*Gospel Advance* is Alvin Reid's challenge to the Church to re-cover our mission focus and advance a movement of God through the gospel. Reading this book is like sitting down across from this passionate evangelism professor and hearing from his heart. He describes the history of evangelical awakenings and prescribes a way forward for 21st century believers. May the Lord use this work to ignite your heart for the nations!"

TREVIN WAX
Managing Editor of *The Gospel Project*
Author of *Counterfeit Gospels*

SOUND WORDS

LISTENING TO THE SCRIPTURES

By Jeremy Carr

"The church continues to need an understanding of discipleship that draws people to love and know God. This book delivers. It is an accessible and practical theology of scripture for discipleship. Jeremy is not exhorting you to love the Bible more, but declaring that God's love for you causes you to know and love him and his Word more."

JUSTIN S. HOLCOMB
Adjunct Professor of Theology and
Philosophy, Reformed Theological Seminary

NOTES

NOTES

NOTES

NOTES

NOTES

NOTES

NOTES

NOTES

NOTES

NOTES

NOTES

NOTES

Made in the USA
Lexington, KY
22 October 2015